Lost

david carson

Lost
@David Carson

A Carson Group Book
ISBN: 978-0-359-69519-5

carsonskc@gmail.com

ONE

I sat behind the bars of the Big Screen in the Racket Nest watching the thin crowds of derelicts drift up and down Broadway, while occasionally an illustrated or penetrated cool boy or girl would go through the door of the tattoo parlor across the street. I decided it was finally time to write Aunt Julie, something I had been putting off for a long time. I took a blank piece of paper out of one of the manila folders I had inherited from my old law school, "Brownback, Kobach, and Klein Y.M.C.A. Night Law School", when it went out of business, and put the paper in front of me on the bar. The light coming through the Big Screen was perfect for composing a letter:

"Dear Aunt Julie,

I'm sorry it's taken me nearly 70 years to reply to your wonderful descriptions of the homestead down on the Cherokee Plains. I miss your garden, pigs, chickens, milk and egg businesses, Percherons, wood stoves, coal-oil lamps, Guinea hens, chamber pots, and wind-up phones. I hope you will forgive my clumsy attempts at writing; I could never match your command of the language even though I have a long and incredibly expensive college education and you only had a grade school education up to the third grade. Of course education has really fallen apart in the century since you went to school. The other day I went looking for the pickup truck I use in the delivery trade here in the city, and it was not in its usual spot. Of course I was very upset and spent much of the day looking for my lost truck; but fortunately I ran into my deep acquaintance, Jason Sloan, who was kind enough to remind me I had wrecked it the day before. Now I am out of work again and in danger of losing my apartment. My landlord is very happy rich suburban idiots are moving into this part of the city, allowing him to move his outrageous rents ever higher; not that his apartment was ever a home to me. You had a real home; I have never had a home here in the city; I wonder if anyone here actually has a home. There are 42 evictions a day in the city, and even landlords are under the thumb of the tax man who must have his way and his wars. I really envy you and your home."

"What do you think you're doing?" asked Jason, who had snuck up behind me in his best undercover way.

"I'm writing my Aunt Julie a letter," I said.

"Where's your cell-phone?"

"At home."

"How can you write a letter?"

"I write long-hand, cursive, with a pen."

"No one writes like that anymore."

"Anything you write on a smart-phone goes straight into the spook machines; the spooks know everything ever written on a smart-phone or a computer," I grumped.

"Well, you should get on your computer or smart-phone more; maybe even you would learn something."

"Like what?"

"The President is converting to Judaism and will hold a mass conversion this Monday; but if you don't want to be Jewish you can leave the country unmolested, but without the right of return."

"Where did you see that?"

"It was on the web, I forget where."

"Pen and paper are not infested with spooks or conversion bullshit."

"You're a Luddite!!"

"So?"

TWO

I held a part-time position working for Jason as a detective, although virtually all my money came from the delivery business. In addition, the delivery business was a lot more interesting than snooping around on people and sticking your nose where it didn't belong; not that I'm not a real tough guy like all those other tough detectives. I'm just not that interested in Jason's business, which includes industrial espionage, missing persons, divorce cases, spying and general snooping. Every day in the delivery business was different with various new stops, new construction mud holes to visit, new factories and warehouses to explore looking for someone who would actually take the responsibility to sign the log, slaughter houses where absolutely no one spoke any English. The delivery trade was not cut and dried like the detective trade; but I was out of business without a truck.

Jason had his own detective business located in the Crossroads, and was also Dean of Drones at our local city college, which boasted the best basketball team in the region. The team always ranked in the top ten within the empire, just as the city always ranked in the top ten in homicides. Jason also worked for his wealthy uncle, Harry Sloan who was chancellor of the local college and the 20ᵗʰ. largest manufacturer of drones in North and South America. Jason evidently hated working for his uncle as much as I hated working for Jason, a suburban twit if there ever was one.

"I can get you a job with real benefits at the college," Jason offered, no doubt out of the kindness of his heart.

"Doing what?"

"How about Assistant Dean of Drones? There's space in my budget for another half dozen assistant deans.

"What does an Assistant Dean of Drones do?"

"Whatever I can think up," smirked Jason, which was actually what I dreaded.

"No thanks."

"How about a position on the campus police force?"

"I don't want to walk around the campus all day long in a ridiculous uniform."

"How are you going to pay me back then?" said Jason. I could see I had to accept something.

"Do you have a campus detective in charge of security?" I asked.

I was hired on the spot as an undercover detective in charge of campus security. Jason went on to brag about his ability to find jobs for people, jobs for nearly anyone at all. He told me he had even found a position for his girl friend Molly as an assistant Dean. Jason had to be a master of conjuring the devil; as soon as he mentioned Molly she appeared through the front door of the Racket Nest in all her glory. She had such an angular, bony face she appeared to have a long snout like a dog; and, as far as I was concerned there was no doubt she was a real bitch. She wrinkled her snout in my direction and said, " I thought I smelled something unpleasant."

"Arf, arf," I said.

" Molly is now the Dean of Political Science, Psychology, Gender Studies, Women Studies, and some thing else I can't remember," bragged Jason.

"Non-white Studies," volunteered Molly.

"Oh yes, Non-white Studies," said Jason.

"Non-white Studies? You have to be kidding," I said.

"Are you a racist?" snarled Molly.

"No, not at all."

"Not only do you stink, you're a failure as a white man," declared Molly.

"Maybe I should get a set of clip-on dreadlocks and try my luck as a non-white man," I said.

"You're a Snark," sneered Molly.

"Snarks are actually Boojums," I said, "what are Non-white Studies?"

"Non-white Studies include everything that's not white supremacist and racist, everything that's not like mathematics, physics, or engineering."

"Mathematics is racist?" I couldn't believe any of her garbage; I couldn't imagine what she was using as a mind.

"Why does one plus one have to be two, why can't one plus one be three? Why are you so narrow-minded, why are you so racist."

"But one plus one is two!"

"That's Racist-Think."

"One plus one is always two!" I couldn't believe I was arguing over an arithmetical fact.

"You're a racist idiot!" she bellowed. I was about to return the compliment by calling her a c-word; but I remembered I had called her the c-word before and she had split my lip with a truly amazing right cross. I'm probably far tougher than the ordinary, run-of-the-mill detective, but discretion is the better part of valor and I could see no reason to expose myself to her formidable right cross again.

I know detectives who use the c-word, the f-word, and the n-word all the time; but that's not tough or strong, that's just d-word stupid. Fortunately my girl friend Meridee swirled through the door and we hurried down to the other end of the bar away from Jason and his lovely inamorata.

THREE

I had to go down to Jason's office in the Crossroads to get a complete idea of my duties as a campus dick. Jason's office was in an office building holding dozens of other small and struggling businesses, which could only afford one receptionist, but could not afford enough to pay her to remain for any length of time. Therefore, a parade of beauties strutted behind the receptionist's desk over the years. The current beauty was a Miss Coplik who had placed an autographed picture of Rachel Madcow in a prominent part of her desk so that everyone could enjoy it. Miss Coplik was reading Hillary's latest book about her political misadventures.

"I see you like satire," I said by way of introducing myself.

"Satire?" she said.

"Madcow and Hillary have to be our greatest satirists, don't you agree?" I said.

"What?", she said as her pleasant smile dissolved into a frown.

"Their defenses of the establishment are so preposterous they can only be satires, don't you agree?"

"What do you want?" she muttered as her pretty face became a hideous snarl, like something on a Japanese samurai about to cut someone's head off.

"I guess political satire became obsolete when Henry Kissinger was awarded the Nobel Peace Prize," I said quoting Tom Lehrer. I just couldn't leave well enough alone, and should have known better than to poke this particular bear.

"What?" she demanded.

"I mean political satire is impossible in this country; it's too far down the toilet vortex," I began to flounder in the face of her outrage. I'm a very tough guy, but I must say, a woman's outrage is hard to face, even for a tough guy like me.

"This is the strongest country in the world," she pronounced.

"Not really, we lost both those world wars, at least spiritually."

"I'm going to call the police," she said, picking up her phone.

I could see discretion would be the better part of valor again, so I scooted past her desk and hurried down the hall to Jason Sloan Investigations where I found Harry Sloan, Jason's filthy rich uncle in conference with Jason.

Jason sat behind his large Formica covered desk in his best suburban suit complete with his long hey-I'm pointing- at-my-crotch length tie while Harry was dressed as a down-and-out clown with a three day beard and tousled hair. As I walked through the door Jason's phone started playing the Star Spangled Banner.

"Hello," said Jason, "yes, he's here right now. No, no, it's all right. No, he's not dangerous. No, please don't call the police, Miss Coplik. There's no reason to call the police, I was expecting him. No, no, he's not a security threat, there's no reason to call the F.B. I. Yes, I'll vouch for him. Thank you, Miss Coplik."

"Thanks, Jason," I said.

"What were you doing with our receptionist?"

"I'm afraid I was committing thought crimes again."

"I've warned you about doing that."

"I can't help it."

"Why do you put up with someone like this?" Harry asked Jason. Harry was not one of my fans and had good reason to dislike me.

"He's my number one detective," said Jason. I was number one all right; I was number two and number last too. Jason hated working for his uncle as much as I hated working for Jason.

"Yes," said Harry; "but how much do I pay him monthly?"

Jason mentioned an extremely small number and maintained he paid me.

"What! Are you trying to bankrupt me?" demanded Harry.

"You told me you were worth 635 million last week," countered Jason.

"Yes, and at this rate I'll go bankrupt before I ever get to a billion. Do you have any idea how much money I owe?"

"Don't you borrow all your money from one of your banks or insurance companies?"

"Yes, but I have to pay it back at some point."

"I have a book titled "The Best Way To Rob A Bank Is To Own One"."

"Do you think I'd actually rob my own bank?"

"I guess not," Jason backed down abjectly, and Harry turned to me and told me to investigate Dr. Hobbs, who was stirring up trouble on campus again through the nefarious Freethought Society, and to find the pyromaniacs setting all the fires in the chemistry, physics, and mathematics buildings. I had my marching orders.

FOUR

I had my marching orders and I didn't like them at all: investigating a well-meaning contrarian and random fires set by some kind of academic nutballs. I didn't want to go back to my nonexistent law practice and confront all those other legal sharks with big debts and small morals. My best bet was to borrow enough money to buy another pickup truck and get back into the delivery business, so I went down to my bank on the Plaza where I had been banking ever since I returned to the city from the Ozarks. I told one of the tellers I was interested in a truck loan and was directed to a desk with a cop sitting behind it, which I thought was a little odd. The name plate on the desk read Bob Perish. I couldn't help myself; I had to ask the loan officer why he was dressed as a cop.

"I am a cop, I didn't have time to change," said Bob.

"You have to work as a cop too to make ends meet?" I was flabbergasted. I thought all bankers had money.

"I'm a pro bono cop. I don't draw a salary, I do it to contribute to the community and because I enjoy it."

"You enjoy being a cop?" I was even more flabbergasted than before.

"Sure, you might consider it yourself."

"I can't be a cop, I'm an officer of the court, I graduated nunca cum laude from the Brownback, Kobach, & Klein Y.M.C.A. Night Law School," I bragged.

"Lawyers can be cops too, although I don't think they should be allowed to be cops."

"Why not?"

"I don't like our legal system; all this precedent stuff gives far too much power to judges and lawyers. And all the judges are lawyers too."

For some reason this really set me off. I wanted to turn over his desk or grab him by the back of the neck and pound his face into his desk. After all, I'm a tough guy; but a tough guy with good manners. Therefore I said, "English common law is better than cop law!"

"I doubt it. Why are you sitting at my desk?"

I explained that I needed a loan to buy a new truck and that I had received a loan at this bank before to buy my last truck.

"Fine," he said and fetched dozens of forms out of his credenza, or is it cadenza? I can't remember.

"What's this?" I asked, "Last time I only filled out one form and had the money immediately."

"This is the information of a good accountant who can help you fill out the forms," Bob said, handing me a fancy embossed business card.

"But there was only one form before?"

"This bank is now a subsidiary of Triple Mega Bank of New York; we do everything according to the latest regulations. Half of the officers you see on the floor here are compliance officers, most of the forms in your stack have to do with compliance."

"Triple Mega?"

"Triple Mega."

"Isn't that one of the banks that was bailed out by the government printing trillions of dollars?"

"Yes, we are a very important institution that can't fail."

"Isn't the government going bankrupt because it's been printing all those trillions?"

"So?"

"It doesn't bother you that the government is going broke?"

"Governments go broke all the time; governments are allowed to go broke."

"You're not allowed to go broke?"

"Of course not! We might bankrupt the future, but we will never go broke."

"Well, I'm not allowed to go broke either!" I said.

'Oh, student loans?" sneered Bob.

I thumbed through the high stack of forms Bob had given me.

"This is an affidavit saying I will not smoke any marijuana until the loan is paid in full?" I asked.

"Yes."

"And this is an affidavit pledging that I have never conspired in any way to overthrow the government?"

"Of course."

"And this is a pledge of allegiance to the flag of the U.S. and the nation for which it stands?"

"Yes."

"What does any of this have to do with a loan for a pickup?"

"It's all compliance; as I mentioned, half of the officer on this platform are compliance."

I could see I was not going to get any loan out of Triple Mega; I was not going to get any loan ever. I slouched out of the bank and resigned myself to working as a lowly campus dick.

FIVE

My first assignment as a lowly campus dick was to figure out what kind of noxious ideas were coming out of that rotten philosophy teacher, Dr. Hobbs, via the Freethought Society. Dr. Hobbs was giving a lecture at the society meeting the next Sunday; I went to the meeting as myself since I saw no reason to disguise myself. I had been to the meetings in the past when Harry Sloan was afraid Hobbs was trying to stir up a general teacher's strike and take over Harry's position as chancellor. As before the meeting was full of do-gooders, people who could easily solve all the problems of the world but could hardly cope with their day-to-day lives. However there were never enough do-gooders around, so I was grudgingly accepted back in the group in spite of my skepticisms and bad attitude.

"So," said Dr. Hobbs as he shook my hand, "the return of the Wyandotte County Twit."

I sat down on the front row of the classroom where the Freethought Society held its lectures like any ass-kissing straight A student. I suspected a lot of the do-gooders were ex-A ass-kissers and brown noses who enjoyed it so much they were continuing the joys of ass-kissing into and beyond their middle ages. Actually I sat on the back row when I had the misfortune to pile up my unpayable school debts. However, my current class-work required a more diligent and respectful approach. Although I'm very intelligent I have trouble with mechanical devices such as can openers and pencil sharpeners; and I hoped Hobbs did not notice me fiddling with my recording device right in front of him.

"First, I'd like to start with a little history from a slightly different point of view than is usual," Hobbs began. Hobbs did not use any of the audiovisual devices or Powerpoint used by normal lecturers who read their lectures off a screen that is plainly visible to all the unfortunates unlucky enough to attend their lectures. Perhaps most lecturers don't believe anybody stupid enough to be in their audiences is capable of reading. Hobbs did not even use any notes or prompters; it was always a scary performance.

"As you all know," Hobbs continued, "this country won both world wars and became very wealthy and powerful; but how, exactly, did we win these two world wars? We won the first world war because we didn't get into it until very late until all the other major fighters had exhausted themselves and run up vast debts with our banks and merchants; and we won the second world war because we didn't get into until very late until all the other major fighters had exhausted themselves and run up vast debts with our banks and merchants. And why didn't we get into these wars until very late? First of all, we live in the Americas, a world away from Eurasia, the center of human population and wealth; and, in both cases, we had very active and vocal groups wisely advocating peace, isolation, and non-intervention. We suffered little of the destructions of war; and our manufacturers and merchants, all the benefits. Last one in always wins. We won those wars because of our unsuccessful peaceniks.

Our elites decided we had won those wars because we are an exceptional nation with an even more exceptional military, and that these wars had saved us from deep depression and economic disaster; therefore they poured ever more money and prestige into the military. Now we are never the last one in, now we are always the first one in; and all the peaceniks are either jailed or silenced using clever psychological warfare, total media control, and unrestrained fear mongering with boogie men from Russians to towel-headed terrorists. We win all the battles and lose all the wars just like the English.

Fortunately for our large military machine and its even larger retinue of camp followers of various kinds there are always plenty of wars to entice all kinds of cool military adventures, and plenty of advocates for each war since our population is largely composed of transients and transplants from various Eurasian diasporas, many of which have large chips on their shoulders because of past slights, injustices, and genocides. Without the very active help of these diasporas it would probably be impossible to keep our perpetual, permanent wars grinding away forever and ever. The warfare state would be impossible.

We even have an active part of the warfare state here on campus: the Drone Department. The Drone Department specializes in training drone pilots, specialized psycho-killers killing at a distance, a very long distance. It even has a program to try to automate the psycho-killers. The head of the Drone Department is Jason Sloan who has been elevated to Assistant Dean.

The end result of the warfare state is bankruptcy as its military starts wars all over the planet and keeps them going as long as possible. The object is never victory, the object is perpetual war. To avoid the worse parts of national bankruptcy we must form a new political organization dedicated to minding our own business, dedicated to finally coming home while we still have a home. I call the new Party the Deplorables. Join us, join the Deplorables now!!"

Hobbs finished his speech to a modest round of applause, and opened his briefcase and spread out several T-shirts on the table in front of him. The shirts read 'Deplorables, Come Home'. I was the only one to buy a shirt, and only two others in the audience signed up on Hobbs's mailing list. The members of the Freethought Society liked to go to a meeting, get thoroughly outraged, then go home and do exactly nothing.

The next day I played my recording back to Jason and Harry Sloan. Harry happened to be back in town to appear in court in a trial involving his cab company. I made a point of wearing my new Deplorables, Come Home T-shirt. Both of the Sloans were very upset with my recording.

"He's obviously a Russian agent!" said Harry.

"A very dangerous man!" said Jason.

"He can't be allowed to teach or lecture; there have to be laws against this kind of thing," said Harry.

"He's only allowed to teach in one of the prisons in Leavenworth County," I said.

"He shouldn't even be allowed to teach there," said Harry.

"Don't we have free speech in this country?" I wondered.

"Yes, but only within reason, for God's sakes!" said Harry.

"He actually thinks we are training psycho-killers?"

"Yes."

"He must be out of his mind. All of our students are citizens and virtually all of them are from one of the nicer suburbs around here, nice people from nice families," said Jason.

"Exactly," I said.

SIX

Jason arranged an official office for me as the official campus dick and a part-time assistant dick named Joe Schultz. The official office was not much bigger than a closet; as a matter of fact it probably had been a closet in the very near past, maybe a week ago. Since Joe and I were to share a very cramped space, I thought it would be only polite to know a little about Joe.

"So," I said, "you're just part time."

"Yes. The drone office only had enough in the budget for a part-time assistant."

"Do you have another job?"

"Of course, I drive for Over."

"Over? The cab company from Monopoly Valley in California?"

"Yes."

"Do you have to use your own car?"

"Yes."

"I understand Over hires literally thousands of drivers here in the city."

"I suppose it does."

"How could anybody working for 'Over' make any money at all?"

"Well, it's better than working for Sloan Cabs; they're a monopoly, you know."

"I know. Tucker law firm had the city rig all the cab regulations in their favor; but anyone can make a living working for Sloan."

"I make money with 'Over'."

"Besides, 'Over' cab is just another monopoly play out of Monopoly Valley; at least it's not as bad as Hercules, the big retail corporation that loses money all the time but has all those black-money, secret contracts with the Deep State."

I could see I was wasting my time again in futile argument. I had told Meridee not to take the job Jason offered her in the Drone Department because she was bound to run into Jason's girl friend Molly. Molly and Meridee had periodic, very violent fights in the Racket Nest. As a matter of fact, those were some of the few violent fights I've ever seen in a city bar. The city is not nearly as violent as it used to be when it was on the eastern edge of the wild, wild West, though, of course we still have the occasional shootings in the schools, shopping malls, churches, grocery stores, and filling stations. Meridee told me she was not afraid of that c-word Molly, and that I was wasting my time arguing against her taking such a high paying job.

"What do you want me to do, Boss," Joe Schultz said to me. I puffed up with pride; no one had ever called me Boss before. At the same time, I was totally lost. I had no idea what to tell Joe. My previous undercover work had been limited to some easy spying at Tucker Law, the local fixers. They rigged elections, told the winners who to appoint to all the various agencies and departments, and told the winners what to do. One of the worst things that can happen to anyone in this city is to be a winner.

"Well," I stammered, "there's a bunch of fires we need to investigate."

"Fires?"

"Explosions too; in the chemistry, physics, and engineering buildings." I was afraid Joe was going to ask me how to go about investigating these fires, but instead he said:

"I'll look into it right away. I used to be a security guard at the county fair, and I know all about this kind of thing."

"Thank God," I thought. I had no idea how anyone should proceed with that kind of investigation. I smiled and congratulated myself. I had become a real Boss at last.

I didn't have long to bask in my new self-importance, after Joe left to investigate the campus fires, Jason called and ordered me to accompany him and Harry Sloan to an important meeting with the Area Transportation Authority. I was very irritated; I had nothing to do with the Area Transportation Authority other than riding in their buses and I knew nothing about them aside from the pile of bus schedules on my table.

"Does this have to do with buses?" I wondered.

"Of course not," said Jason, "it has to do with Sloan Cab."

"I can't afford cabs."

"Don't you still have that recording device I gave you?"

"Yes."

"Well, wire yourself for sound and come with me to the meeting in 30 minutes."

"Why?" I asked out of irritation. It was bad news to order someone around who had just become a real Boss.

"Harry wants a recording of the entire meeting," demanded Jason.

Actually I found the meeting with the commissioners of the transport authority to be very interesting. The Tucker attorneys were able to get nowhere against the monopoly charges against Sloan Cab argued by Over's California attorneys. Perhaps the Tucker boys and girls were specialists in different brands of corruption than Monopoly Valley corruption; but Harry Sloan himself took up the argument:

"Monopoly, monopoly.....that's rich coming from these bastards," began Harry.

"Everything that comes out of Monopoly Valley is designed to be a monopoly or at least part of a very tight cartel. Didn't it used to be against anti-trust laws to demolish competition by taking loses only a billionaire could afford? Didn't it used to be against the law to finance entire cartels with black money, secret contracts with government goons and spooks? Over is a monopoly play on a worldwide basis. Over floods every city with thousands of drivers since they bear no cost for cars or benefits. None of their drivers will ever be able to make a living; at least my drivers can make a living if they put in the hours," finished Harry.

The commissioners huddled briefly and decided in favor of Over. As we left the conference room, Harry turned

and shouted, "I'll get my own goddamn computer application!"

SEVEN

Next day I was back in my new office by myself since Joe had the day off to drive the city for Over. It was a great luxury to sit in my office alone and do absolutely nothing; however, I was not given very long to do absolutely nothing. The phone rang.

"Hello," I said.

"My name is Jaybird Bolton, head of student loans. We must do something about all the threatening letters and calls I get."

"I don't see why that's my business," I said.

"You're in charge of campus security!"

"I am? I'm the campus dick. I don't have anything to do with campus security."

"Jason Sloan's office, someone named Meridee, said you were in charge of security. In case you didn't know, Jason Sloan is a Dean of this university."

"I'll get right back to you," I said, and hung up on him to

call Jason, who told me it was part of my duty to handle security. I was totally lost. My previous undercover work had been limited to some easy spying at Tucker Law, the local fixers. They rigged elections, told the winners who to appoint to all the various agencies and departments, and told the winners what to do. One of the worst things that can happen to anyone in this city is to be a winner.

I had to go over to the student loan office and confront Jaybird Bolton myself, which was certainly no fun at all. He was a very stern older man with white hair and an impressive white walrus moustache that hid his mouth so that his strained voice appeared to come straight out of his moustache. He sat behind an impressive walnut desk under the head of a giraffe mounted on the wall. About 10 feet of the giraffe's neck extended from the head back into the wall.

"That's an impressive giraffe," I said by way of starting the conversation, while wondering what kind of asshole would shoot a giraffe.

"My grandfather, the famous judge here in the city shot it," strained out of the moustache.

"How very nice," I lied, while remembering that almost all the judges in this city were infamous, not famous.

"So you're in charge of security?" asked the moustache.

"Yes." I could see he was not very impressed by my physical presence, though most people are not very impressed by my physical presence either.

"Is that all you have to say?" blared out of the moustache. I suddenly felt I was the subject of an intense interrogation, perhaps one of those enhanced interrogations.

"Not only did you hang up on me, you didn't even know that you were in charge of security!" continued the moustache.

"I apologize for hanging up on you."

"What about security?"

"What about it?"

"What are you going to do about it?"

"Here I am, talking to you. What seems to be the problem?"

"I've been receiving all these anonymous threats over the campus internet."

"So?"

"What do you mean, 'So'?"

"So what do you want me to do about it?" I had enough of his nonsense; apparently idiocy ran in his family.

An incredible rant emerged from the moustache; I wish I was still wired in order to record all it, but I had given the recording device to Joe Schultz. What I can remember was something like this:

"There is nothing as important as security. Security keeps us alive; security saves us from all the dangers that throng this world. We are protected by security as we walk through this valley of the shadow of death. Security is hydra-headed; there is local security, state security, and above all, national security. There is campus security and you, you idiot, have no idea what it is."

I knew from our first meeting that we were not going to get along, and I was prepared to put up with Mr. Jaybird Bolton to the best of my ability. However, being called an idiot by an idiot was more than I could manage in a smooth manner.

"You're scared shitless, aren't you?" I muttered, and everything changed entirely for no reason at all. Every now and then the eternal cycle of the hours, of the seasons and years is thrown off-track by something unexpected and unexplained, something from a different reality.

Two loud shots were fired close to my head, and someone behind me bellowed, "On the floor assholes, face down!" Everyone in the office, including Jaybird Bolton and myself obeyed quickly. I am probably far tougher and courageous than virtually anyone; but as we all know, discretion is the better part of valor. Therefore I lay on the floor, face-down.

"Who's in charge here?" bellowed the voice from nowhere that could be seen, "Who saddled me with all these debts I can't possibly pay. I can't even take bankruptcy!"

I felt like telling him it was Bolton, but a perverse sense of decency held me back, a disaster as I was to learn later. He could have shot Bolton and solved a lot of problems.

Next we heard a loud female voice demand, "What are you doing with that gun? You know you're not allowed on campus!!" It was Molly herself. Evidently she snatched the gun away from our attacker, because the next thing she said was: "Now get out of here before I report you to campus police. Why don't all you chickenshits get up now?"

I stumbled to my feet and manfully met the full, and terrible glare of Molly, a person with no discretion at all, therefore not really a courageous person.

"I see the campus police are already here. How do you expect to do your job face-down on the floor?"

"I don't carry a gun," I said mildly, and in a very reasonable way.

"Here's his gun. Can't you afford a gun?"

"I don't believe in carrying a gun."

"Why not?"

"I don't believe in violence."

"You're the campus dick, and you don't believe in violence?" sneered Molly.

EIGHT

After all the excitement at the loan office I was happy to retreat to my closet office and spend some time meditating, or just sitting there alone looking at the walls. Of course there were no windows in my office. In order to jazz my office up a little I brought a big color picture of Yosemite Park I had rolled up in my apartment to the office and put it up on the wall. Unfortunately there was not enough wall to hold the picture, so I had to wrap it around one corner of the office. But that looked a little strange; Yosemite bending around a corner in a room. I hit on a brilliant solution, if I do say so myself, and I do. I decided to frame the picture. Since the frame had to go around the corner too with the picture it took some virtuoso carpentry on my part and several days to finish the frame. Just as I finished the frame Joe Schultz came in the office to see me. I have to confess I was surprised because I had forgotten he was working for me.

"What's up?" I said.

Good news, Boss. I have pictures of the person planting the bombs in the engineering building. I went through all the security camera files on campus and found these pictures."

"Great," I said, pretending to be interested. I had also forgotten we were supposed to be investigating the campus bombings.

"Here they are," said Joe spreading several pictures of the back of some woman's head on my desk.

"Joe, these are pictures from the back."

"I couldn't find any others," said Joe. I could see he was disappointed by my reaction, "but at least they're in color."

"I had no idea we had color surveillance cameras," I said.

"Jason Sloan himself insisted we install color security systems."

"The bomber has striking auburn hair," I muttered. There was something disturbing about the bomber's hair; and it was especially disturbing that I couldn't figure out what was disturbing about it. It was like trying to forget something unpleasant that keeps trying to pop back into mind in spite of all efforts.

"Thanks, Boss. I'll look into it right away," said Joe. Actually it would have been fine with me if he didn't look into it, but in the circumstances I felt I shouldn't say anything. Joe left and I fixed myself a pot of coffee to help with my contemplation of Yosemite going around the corner of my room. It was very pleasant again. Certainly the philosopher who said all the problems of the world are caused by our inability to sit peacefully in our rooms was correct. I spent the rest of my day sitting peacefully in my room, hoping Joe stayed out of trouble.

But Joe didn't stay out of trouble; he was back the next day with another stack of photos.

"I went down to the F.B.I. office here in the city, showed them my credentials as a campus dick, and they were very helpful. They have a complete file on the hair color of all the women in this area including photographs. Their forensic lab was able to find 24 matches to the auburn hair of the bomber; and here they are," gushed Joe excitedly.

"Calm down, take it easy Joe," I said. I could see no reason to get excited over women with auburn hair. Joe laid the photos out on my desk. One of them was Molly.

"There must be mistake," I said.

"Why?" asked Joe, "this is the work of the F.B.I.!"

"That doesn't mean anything."

"What? But Boss, the F.B.I. is famous."

"You mean infamous," I said, "the F.B.I. makes mistakes all the time."

"I don't see any mistakes here," said Joe.

"This is a picture of Molly, a woman I know. She is an Assistant Dean of Humanities at this college. I can't imagine an assistant dean bombing her own college, can you?"

"I didn't know," said Joe. I could see he was very disappointed, crestfallen.

"Don't worry about it. Here's the Walther Molly snatched from the lunatic in student loans. See if you can trace it; see where a lunatic might get a pistol like this."

"Why, you can buy guns like that at any sports goods store in town, you can even buy machine guns."

"Yes, but see if you can trace this particular gun."

"O.K. Boss," Joe took the gun and left me in peace contemplating Yosemite running around the corner of my office. I realized that Joe was a far better detective than I could ever hope to be; that I should rely on him to conduct all our investigations. Due to my generous and magnanimous nature I was even willing to give Joe partial credit for everything we did in spite of his gross handicap of only having a high school degree from a low grade high school, Wyandotte High, in a blue collar part of the city. Joe reminded me of Paula, who showed she was a much better attorney than I even though she only had a third grade education. Both Joe and Paula take unfair advantage of their natural talents, which were not granted to me.

Sometimes people allow their natural talents carry them away. I guess Joe couldn't help it, couldn't control his detective nature, his mania to analyze and over-apply logic. The next day he interrupted me again while I was drinking coffee, finishing a nice powdered donut, and contemplating Yosemite running around the corner.

"Good news, Boss," Joe began. I instinctively dreaded hearing his new discoveries.

"What's up?" I said, pretending to be cool, and very nonchalant.

"That pistol didn't go through any normal channels. I went down to the offices of Homeland Security in the city, and once they knew I was a campus dick, they helped me trace that gun. It comes from a criminal shipment of arms from Russia into the bookstore on our campus. Also, I have a surveillance photo of the receiving clerk at the time."

Joe whipped one of his photos out; again it was a photo of the back of the head of some woman with striking auburn hair.

"Doesn't that look familiar?" asked Joe.

"No, not really," I said.

"It has to be Molly," said Joe.

"Impossible!" I said.

NINE

I decided I needed a drink; I had been neglecting my drinking habit, which had a very bad effect on my normal good temper and sharp intellect. However, as soon as I entered the Racket Nest I regretted it. I ordered the most innocuous beer I could think of from Ted, the bartender, who immediately launched into a dismal diatribe about the city forcing all the bartenders to pass a city exam in sexual harassment.

"But why are you upset?" I asked, "I always thought you were very good at sexual harassment, one of the very best."

"You don't understand," grumped Ted.

Before I could reply I was assaulted by Molly who had been lurking in wait at the end of the bar.

"Why if it isn't Mr. Chickenshit the campus dick himself," she sneered as she flounced her head to show off her auburn hair.

"Who was that guy at the student loan office? I said.

"That was one of my students in gender studies; I should say, he used to be a student of mine in gender studies," she said.

"Gender studies?"

"You wouldn't understand; I don't think you could possibly understand," maintained Molly.

"Why was he attacking the student loan office with that gun?"

"I cut him off, I cut him off at the knees!"

"You cut him off at the knees?"

"Yes, I made it impossible for him to take his credits anywhere else and capped his student loan amount so he couldn't borrow any more money."

"Why?"

"He wouldn't wear the red high heeled shoes to class; he actually had to nerve to say it was a ridiculous requirement."

"You demanded your male students wear high heeled shoes to class?"

"Of course!"

"Are you out of your mind?"

"The idea is to demonstrate to the stupid male creature just how hard it is to walk in high heeled shoes."

"I like come-fuck-me shoes on a good looking tomato," I volunteered, "but on a guy they're ridiculous."

"You are a moron, a failure as a white man," said Molly.

"Yes, why be a man if you can be a success?" I said, quoting some German commie whose name I can't remember.

"I'm both a woman and a success! I'm a professor, dean of the college, and sit on the board of trustees."

"Your married boyfriend, Jason, gave you those positions."

"Yes, but all he did for you was make you a campus dick. I bet you're not capable of being a private dick. I bet you'll never be anything but a campus dick."

"Sure, I could be a private detective if I wanted."

"You're too chickenshit!" she sneered.

I had an urge to cold cock her right there; put her down with an unexpected haymaker. But I'm a gentleman after all, and gentlemen do not hit ladies, not that Molly was any kind of lady. Also, I remembered that Molly had a wicked right cross, and could usually hold her own with my girl friend Meridee for at least a minute or so. It would really look bad if Molly were able to knock the crap out of me. I would get no sympathy at all.

Molly turned away from me and strutted back to her end of the bar; I have to admit she can strut better than virtually any chicken in the barnyard. "You should see her strut!", as the song goes.

My flip phone rang as she strutted away with an urgent call from Jason, who was down at his detective office in the crossroads with his uncle who had just returned from a trip to his financiers in New York. Jason requested my appearance at his office in order to deal with his uncle who was evidently having one of his periodic anxiety attacks about bankruptcy. Although Harry Sloan claimed he was worth 653 million dollars, he also claimed he was on the verge of a total bankruptcy again. Jason had kept his office in the crossroads in case his uncle actually did declare bankruptcy, and the city college had to follow him soon after. There's nothing like a good bankruptcy to clear the air and sort things out.

By the time I reached Jason's office the air was thick and Harry was in a panic, pacing up and down in Jason's office and muttering, "They turned me down, they turned me down again! I can't believe it, they turned me down!"

"What seems to be the problem here?" I said mildly in my most reasonable way.

"They won't loan him any money to pay his latest interest bill; they may not renew his loans," said Jason.

"That's not the worst of it," moaned Harry, who looked as if he had been dragged through a knothole and given a solid beating.

"He can't join their club," said Jason with a faint smirk. I could see he enjoyed his uncle's pain, and saw nothing wrong with indulging in schadenfreude at a relative's expense.

"What club?"

"The Overthrow Club."

"The Overthrow Club?"

"All members in good standing must be billionaires and have overthrown at least one large corporation or one country," said Jason.

"They offered me auxiliary status and a loan at twenty percent if I would put up all my property here in the city," groaned Harry.

"Twenty percent, that's not bad," I said, "I'm paying thirty-six percent on my credit cards and my student loans. Can you declare bankruptcy if you can't pay?"

"Of course."

"I can't; at least not on my student loans."

TEN

Harry went on to explain that the Overthrow Club had excluded him from their very lucrative overseas markets in munitions and drones. He said drone manufacturing was driving him into bankruptcy because he couldn't sell anything to overseas militaries or police. He had to have those markets to make ends meet.

"They would only give me Costa Rica," moaned Harry.

"Costa Rica?" I said.

"Maybe we can sell a lot of drones in Costa Rica."

"Candy is dandy, but liquor in quicker; I could drink all the rum in Costa Ricer," I recited giving away everything I knew about Costa Rica.

"O.K. wise guy, you go down to Costa Rica and try to sell some drones to their military," said Harry, reverting to his normal, nasty self.

"But I'm the head of campus security!"

"I'm sure the board of directors would agree to an extended leave of absence for your trip to Costa Rica," said my pal, my buddy, Jason.

A couple of days later it was time for another talk by Dr. Hobbs at the Freethought Society that infested the college every Sunday. Harry Sloan thought it was very important to monitor all of their talks, and especially the talks given by Dr. Hobbs, who Harry thought was a possible contender for his spot as chancellor of the college. In addition, Harry believed freethought was just another word for thoughtcrime, and charged me with recording and reporting them if at all possible. I have to admit I'm not at all familiar with thoughtcrime laws and statues though I had a very good legal education at the Brownback, Kobach, and Klein Y.M.C.A. Night Law School. For some reason, thoughtcrimes were not part of our curriculum. Therefore, I had to rely on my own judgment and good common sense in that matter.

Dr. Hobbs was selling his T-shirts with the motto "Deplorables, Come Home!" for twenty dollars no doubt as a supplement to his nonexistent income as a philosophy professor restricted to local jails and penitentiaries. Hobbs talk was full of thoughtcrimes of the very worst kind. He said our phony allies dictated our foreign policy, which required the maintenance of hugely expensive military bases all over the world. He said the country had been destroyed in the service of empire, and that there was no home to which we could return. He said that we were not really deplorables, that we just lived in a colony of the colonies on the coasts. He said our leaders were nothing more than very successful crooks totally unhindered by any morals or principles. It was a bonanza of thoughtcrime, though it was hard to pinpoint the crimes exactly, just as it is hard to come up with a good legal definition of terrorism, or of the word 'is'. What is the meaning of 'is'? My God, what a brilliant question!

Meanwhile Joe was pursuing Molly even though I had tried to stop his investigations. Joe even traced her to Jason Sloan; and asked me to go to Jason and ask him if he had any knowledge of Molly's activities. To keep the peace I agreed, and the Monday after Hobbs massive thoughtcrimes I went to Jason's palatial office on campus.

"Do you know what Molly is doing here on campus?" I asked.

"Well, I appointed her to run the humanities department. Every good drone school needs a solid humanities department, don't you think?"

"I guess so," I said lamely. "Say, did you ever wonder why Molly likes to prance, strut, stomp, and scream so much?"

"O, she's been learning flamenco for years now; and goes to practice every Thursday."

I could see I was not getting anywhere with Jason, who also asked when I was going to Costa Rica on a drone sales trip. He said he had made me an Assistant Associate Dean in the Drone Department so I could duly impress our customers in Costa Rica. I gave up asking about Molly.

The next day a guy showed up from the Grounds and Buildings Department to put a sign on my closet saying 'Assistant Associate Dean of Drones'. I wasn't about to put up with that nonsense and told him to take a hike. He shrugged and walked away with his painting gear.

"What's wrong with being Assistant Associate Dean of Drones?" asked Joe.

"Are you kidding?"

"Aren't you supposed to go to Costa Rica to sell some drones?"

"Yeah, sure, but I don't want to go," I said.

"Why not?"

"Do you want to sell drones?" I countered.

"Sure, why not? I'd love to go to Costa Rica."

"O.K., you go in my place," I said automatically without realizing it was actually a very good idea. No doubt Joe was a competent salesman too; and a nice trip would keep him away from campus at least for awhile. I could sit in our office and meditate on the big picture of Yosemite curling around a corner without any interference. I could meditate with the best; but detective work baffled me more often than not.

Next day I took Joe to the airport in our campus cop car that I had labeled campus POLICE. I had considered using it to run deliveries also, but decided that would be unseemly and injurious to the dignity of campus security. However, it was a lot of fun running the siren on the way up to the airport. We made it in record time!

I settled down to an extended meditation, and enjoyed virtually no interruptions though I did doze off several times at my desk during the next few days. I received an e-mail from Joe that read:

"Dear Boss,

Hope you are doing better than I am. The flight south out of Mexico City was in one of those old DC-3 propeller planes. At our first scheduled stop we had to circle the field for 2 hours in a thunderstorm because we were receiving ground fire. Virtually everyone on board was sick in a very messy way. Once I was off the plane I discovered it was the wrong stop, that they were having a revolution, and that the DC-3 was already taxiing down the runway for its next flight. Thank God we have such a great, stable government in the States, and not a lot of political violence. I chased the plane down the runway; but fell into a rather deep ditch, no

doubt because of the free rum served on the DC-3. I
had to spend the night in that tropical ditch, and I didn't
sleep well because I wondered what else might be in
that tropical ditch with me. But I'm doing better today,
and should be in San Jose within the hour. Joe.
P.S. Thanks for making me Special Envoy to Costa Rica
for the Assistant Associate Dean of Drones."

ELEVEN

The next message I received from Joe was more alarming.

"Dear Boss,

Did you know Costa Rica doesn't have any military? All they have are some local militias; they don't even have many police. I understand a lot of towns have disbanded their police and are suffering a big decline in crime and corruption. Thank God our police are mostly hard working heroes of one kind or another. The only people down here who wanted to buy drones don't have any money. I think this was a bum steer! I should be back in the office tomorrow or the next day. Joe."

In addition, my peace and quiet was interrupted by the soccer coach, who rang me up to complain about his balls being stolen. I have to admit I had no idea how to investigate soccer ball theft; but, on the other hand, I had no idea how to investigate explosions in science buildings either. The only pleasant thing about it was the soccer coach, Dick Jones, who seemed to be a very pleasant man, someone who was a joy to all around him. He also seemed to like me too, which I appreciated very much since there are not a lot of people who like me in the least. Dick liked to talk, and even told me that it was hard to manage on a soccer coach's budget, and that the theft of his balls made it even harder. I replied with a soulful rendition of my own troubles with huge student debt. We understood each other.

"It is impossible to declare bankruptcy on student debt," I said.

"Really!" said Dick, "I didn't know that. I've declared bankruptcy several times myself, but just on business loans."

"My God," I said, "I'd love to declare bankruptcy; then I could stop being a campus dick and cruise around the world on a sailboat, or something like that."

"Did you know some soccer coaches make big bucks, I mean really big bucks?" said Dick.

"I thought the big bucks were just for basketball and football."

"O No. A first class soccer school pays its coaches really big bucks."

"This is not a first class soccer school?"

"Are you kidding me? All we have here is some kind of strange drone school. But some soccer schools have such high prestige soccer coaches can get rich selling soccer scholarships to wealthy alums who want to get their kids in the school."

"We get a lot of foreign students here because their governments can pay; but most locals don't have the money."

"They can always borrow the money," said Dick.

"Yeah," I countered, "and wind up like me, a campus dick somewhere." I rolled in self-pity like a hound rolling in shit.

"I'm the lowest paid soccer coach in our conference," groused Dick.

"Well, I'll find your balls!!" I promised, though I had absolutely no idea how to find his stolen balls.

Several days later Joe showed up at the office early enough to interrupt my early morning meditation on Yosemite.

"Good morning, Boss. I brought you a present from Costa Rica." Joe put a clear bottle of some kind of colorless liquid on my desk.

"What's that?"

"It's rum!"

"It doesn't look like rum; it doesn't have a label or any color."

"It's the real thing; it's not one of those manufactured bottles of chemicals they sell around here."

"Let's try some," I suggested.

"Good idea," said Joe.

Although I don't normally drink a lot while I'm on duty, Joe's rum was so smooth and good the two of us drank the whole bottle on the spot. Later that evening Joe became very sick; he blamed it on the rum and unwisely decided to become a teetotaler.

"Say Joe," I said, " what do you think about my picture of Yosemite?"

"Why does it run around the corner?"

"Because the wall is too small."

"No, the picture is too big."

"No, no, the picture is just right; it's the wall that's the wrong size."

"The picture is too big."

"Listen, who's boss here?"

"You are, but the picture is still too big."

We spent the rest of the afternoon arguing about the size of the wall and the picture of Yosemite. By the next day we were both sober enough to not argue about nonsense; instead we argued about some very important stuff, (VIS) for short.

"Joe," I began, "someone is stealing balls from the soccer program. This is something that has to stop. I know the soccer coach personally, and he is extremely upset. I think we should look into it immediately."

"But what about the explosions in the science buildings?"

"That can wait."

"Don't you think explosions in the science buildings, clear acts of terrorism, are more important than some lost soccer balls?"

"Dick Jones tells me the soccer balls were definitely stolen."

"How does he know?"

"Well, because they're not there anymore."

"But couldn't he have misplaced his balls?"

"A soccer coach does not misplace his balls."

"How do you know that's true?" argued Joe. I was beginning to get very annoyed. I didn't want to investigate the explosions because it might implicate my boss, Jason, through his girl friend Molly. I am very sensitive about matters of this kind of etiquette. I decided to outflank Joe with an extraneous bullshit argument.

"The soccer coach, Dick Jones, is a very important guy here on campus. He is the Director of White Dude Day on campus."

"White Dude Day?"

"Yes, it's a weekly event celebrating white dudes."

"Why?"

"Well the women have International Women's Day, and the minorities have International Victim's Day. We need to have a White Dude Day."

Actually Dick Jones had never said anything about a White Dude's Day to me; but I hated to say I thought it up all by myself. I was sure Coach Jones would go along with it, and it turned out, I was right. He thought it was a great idea.

TWELVE

Dick Jones decided to start a White Dude organization right here on campus. I wasn't really in a position to tell him it was not really a good idea because the college depended financially on foreign students who were, by and large, definitely not white dudes since I had come up with the white dude idea in the first place. Within a week Jones had recruited a bedraggled bunch of debt slaves to join his organization; and had even contracted with an inspirational speaker, Paul Craig Robards, to give a promotional speech. Jones plastered the campus with flyers for the Paul Craig Robards speech, which caught the attention of Molly.

One morning I was peacefully meditating with the help of Yosemite, minding my own business and not bothering anyone when Molly pounded on my office door.

"Take down those speech flyers!" she demanded.

"What flyers?" I said. Playing dumb has always been one of my very best strategies, a natural for someone of my abilities.

"Those flyers for that white supremacist piece of shit!"

"Don't we have free speech at this college?"

"Who posted all that garbage!"

"Dick Jones."

"Dick Jones!!!," she barked.

"Yes, Dick Jones the soccer coach."

"I'm the soccer coach!"

"Dick Jones is the soccer coach."

"I'm the women's soccer coach," bragged Molly who was evidently very proud of herself teaching the ladies how to chase an inflated ball all over someone's lawn.

"Dick Jones is also head of White Dudes," I said.

"White Dudes?" sneered Molly, "are you a member too?"

"Yes, I am. Is there something wrong with that?"

"Is there anything right about that?"

"I don't think you qualify to be a member," I said. I try to be diplomatic whenever possible. Campus security is totally different from municipal or national security, and requires a deft, diplomatic touch, an empathetic approach to possible offenders and clients. The idea is not to arrest a lot of people or issue a lot of tickets, but to smooth things out. Molly was very hard to smooth out; but then, she was staff and faculty, not a student.

"You're a male chauvinist pig and a white supremacist," charged Molly who turned away and stomped out of my office. Before I had time to achieve a little piece of mind again, and just as I was slipping into a very satisfying meditation on the picture of Yosemite, Joe barged into our office.

"Good news, Boss," said Joe.

"Oh No," I thought to myself. Good news for Joe was nearly always bad news for me.

"I chipped all the balls."

"You chipped all the balls?"

"Yes, I put little transmitter chips on all of Dick Jones soccer balls so his balls could be traced, just like they put chips in underwear to cut down on shoplifting."

"Wow, that's brilliant," I said even though I could sense this was leading to some kind of very bad news.

"Some of the chipped balls were stolen, just as I hoped."

"So?" I loved the monosyllabic 'so'. I had picked it up from one of my heroes, Dick Cheney.

"So I traced the stolen balls to the girls' soccer team; and you know who's coach of the girls' soccer team?"

"Molly."

"Yes, I'm convinced she's responsible for all the explosions and fires in the physics and math buildings too. We need to bring her in for a good stiff interrogation."

"Joe, her boyfriend, Jason, hired both of us."

"So?" Joe spat Dick Cheney right back at me.

"I don't think it would be good form to interrogate his girl friend."

"What do manners have to do with this; we're talking about right and wrong?"

"Joe, we're not city cops or federal snoops or anything like that. We're campus dicks. Our job is to protect the faculty and the students, to make their stay on our campus a golden time in their memories."

"We can't let that c-word get away with this," demanded Joe.

"All right, I'll talk to her about the ball problem," I conceded. I had to admire Joe's integrity. God knows how or where he got it. But it was totally thankless to argue with Joe; it never led anywhere. For example we even argued about why our leaders are so bad.

"You ever wonder why are Presidents are always so bad?" Joe asked one day.

"They're just front men, anyone knows that," I had said.

"Then why are the folks pulling the strings always so bad?"

"It's in the nature of things."

"What does that mean?"

"If you would meditate every now and then you would understand what I'm talking about."

"I don't need to meditate to fall asleep; I can fall asleep anytime I want."

"What are you talking about?"

"Every time you try to meditate you doze off," Joe had maintained.

THIRTEEN

Anyway, I decided to confront the Molly immediately. There's no reason to procrastinate on the unpleasant, it just makes the unpleasant even worse. I went to Humanities Hall to her lecture Monday morning in American Studies. When I went to college there were no classes called American Studies or Gender Studies or Black Studies or Women Studies; but everything in the social sciences had changed with the times. Molly was already in full spate when I arrived; I slid unobtrusively in an empty chair in the last row.

"Someone has to stop letting white dudes name birds. Every other bird has a ridiculous name, such as nuthatch, sapsucker, booby, woodpecker, or even swallow. And what's worse are the names white dudes give women such as slattern, tart, whore, twat, or even c-word. This has to stop; we have to stop white dudes from framing reality by not using their words. We need to make up our own words and use them. Instead of nuthatch, sapsucker, booby or woodpecker we could say rather large bird that eats things it pecks out of the bark of a tree, or little brown bird that hops around the ground and eats seeds. Instead of slattern, tart, whore, or twat we should say lady forced to sell herself to disgusting men, or unfortunate woman victimized by outrageous white dudes."

Molly finished her slanders of white dudes with a demand that all her students protest the upcoming speech of Paul Craig Robards promoting white dude culture. Next she launched into a far-fetched analysis of truth.

"One of the things we have learned from postmodern American theory is that truth is relative, that absolute truth does not exist, that it has never existed and never will exist. This paradigm is accepted everywhere except for some backward enclaves such as exist right here on campus in our mathematics, physics, and chemistry departments. The backward idiots and morons that infest these disciplines actually believe in absolute truth. For example, the idiots in the math department right here on campus insist that two plus two must always equal four. Under different circumstances, why couldn't two plus two equal five. These idiots are so closed minded they will only accept one answer; they don't understand that truth is relative, that two plus two might be anything. Meanwhile the idiots in the physics department are complicit in the construction of terrible weapons capable of wiping out most of the life on the planet; they are even proud of their immoral, scummy ventures. One of the professors even likes to show off the glass formed in the desert sand by exploding atomic weapons at one of their test sites in New Mexico. We must protest the outrages of Paul Craig Robards and his white dudes; we must protest the outrages committed daily here on campus in the math., physics, and chemistry departments to say nothing about similar idiocies committed in biology, geology, and engineering departments."

She concluded her incredible rant with the observation that all the theories in the social sciences were new and modern instead of old and mouldy like some of the theories used in physical sciences. After her victims filed out of the classroom she came up to me and said:

"Who told you you could audit my class!"

"I'm here on official business," I said.

"Imagine that," she sneered.

"Dick Jones' stolen balls were traced to you."

"I had no balls and Dick Jones had balls!"

"You didn't pay for the balls."

"Of course not, the women's soccer program has no budget, Dick Jones soccer program has a very fat budget."

"You stole his balls," I insisted.

"Why you piece of shit," she said as she swung on me with a vicious right cross. She didn't really hit me very hard; but I was so surprised that I stumbled backwards over a chair and fell. She then proceeded to kick me in the ribs. Fortunately Joe had traced me to Molly's classroom and pulled her off me before she had done more than break a couple of ribs.

"Gosh Boss," Joe said, "You let that little woman kick the shit out of you."

"I try to be a gentleman at all times; how would it look if I were to hit a lady?"

"She's no lady, Boss."

I have a chronic cough from breathing the salubrious air in our city most of my life; and a cough with two broken ribs is a form of torture not to be wished on anyone. Joe and I retreated to our office where I could suffer in peace, meditating on the picture of Yosemite. But Joe would not leave me in peace.

"We need to press charges, Boss, at least for assault and battery but also for theft and grand terrorism."

"Grand terrorism?"

"Because of all the explosions and fires she started."

"We don't have proof."

"Well, I saw her kick the shit out of you, Boss."

"Joe. I don't want it to get around."

"She took advantage of your good nature."

"I still don't want it to get around; it makes me look like a fool."

"Boss, I never worry about looking like a fool."

"Good thing, too."

"Are you worried about Jason Sloan?"

"Yes, what would he think if we pressed charges against his girl friend."

"I think there's something you should know about Mr. Sloan, Boss."

"What?"

"His wife pleasures a whole line of suburban teen-age boys every Saturday night while Sloan is out running around with that Molly person. Here's her picture."

"She's a looker."

"Stone-cold fox.   I was thinking of getting in line myself."

"Where did you get all this information?"

"We're part of the establishment, Boss. As campus dicks we have access to all the local, state, and federal surveillance networks."

"That's disgusting!"

FOURTEEN

After Molly's assault Joe took me to the campus clinic where I was issued some cool pain pills, then returned with me to our small office.

"I'll show you how to get into the surveillance records," Joe offered, out of kindness I suppose.

"Not interested," I said.

"They are a very important tool in police work," said Joe.

"So?"

"We're campus security, campus dicks, cops."

"I prefer to think of myself as an attorney, an officer of the court, with a J.D. from the Brownback, Kobach, and Klein Y.M.C.A. Night Law School."

"Artificial intelligence of the highest order was used to compile the surveillance records."

"So?"

"Well, you know how complex the law is; how it is designed to make sure everyone breaks laws and is therefore a criminal. Since ignorance of the law is no excuse, everyone can be prosecuted," said Joe.

"Yes."

"I even looked up your pre-crime dossier," said Joe.

"What.......Well I have nothing to hide."

"What about your habit of sniffing mustard at the grocery store and then not buying the jar of mustard?"

"Everybody does that."

"What about taking a leak behind billboards?"

"Everybody does that."

"Taking a leak behind billboards is considered a sexual perversion.   You could be on a list of sex perverts."

"What!?"

"And what about the time you were peddling student loans to derelicts in the bus station or outside the welfare office?"

"I have never peddled student loans of any kind to anyone."

"That's not what's in your record," said Joe.

"The record's wrong. What possible connection could there be between all this stuff?"

"Artificial intelligence allows the investigator to weave everything together. Perhaps you were financing your mustard and sex debauches by peddling government loans to fraudulent colleges."

"I want those slanders off my record!!"

"O.K. Boss, I'll print up the expungement papers from Bigly."

"Bigly?"

"Bigly's one of those big Monopoly Valley companies that handle records for Homeland Security."

Joe left the office, but returned about an hour later with a pile of paper several inches thick, which turned out to be expungement papers that required character references from a dozen relatives and two dozen unrelated people, a complete record of all institutions of learning I had attended starting with pre-kindergarten, any military record and record of release from military service, any governmental post of any kind I had held, any non-governmental post of any kind I had ever held, a brief autobiography covering my entire life on a daily basis, any awards of any kind and documentation validating the awards, any ribbons won in athletic competitions, complete medical records from birth. All records were to be validated with sworn affidavits before a notary and five witnesses.

I decided to fill out the papers in order to save my reputation and honor, although I must say, I found the task of writing an autobiography of my entire life on a daily basis a daunting task. I soon ran into a blank wall trying to remember April 10 from 30 years ago. How is it possible to live a life and forget about it at the same time? I just sat in the office for hours looking at the picture of Yosemite with nothing at all on my mind. It wasn't even a meditation. I just sat there with absolutely nothing on my mind.

Suddenly Joe came back into the office.

"Look at this, Boss. I finally captured that bitch from the front." Jason flashed the kind of bad pictures taken by security cameras.

"Who is it?" I said, squinting at the blurred images.

"Molly! It's Molly setting a fire in the physical chemistry lab."

"How can you tell she's setting a fire?"

"It's in the sequence of pictures. Look at this!"

I shuffled through Joe's photos; but failed to see what he could see. However I could see he was obsessing over Molly. As time passed I continued to fill out the expungement papers while Joe continued to build a file on Molly. I didn't say anything about his obsession with Molly, but dreaded the consequences. Molly was the kind of person that always seems to be in charge of every organization, the kind of person who buzzed through any kind of opposition.

I decided to take a break from the expungement papers by recording Dr. Hobbs' lecture at the next Freethought Society meeting. Hobbs was full of fire and brimstone in a direct assault on our college:

"In ancient times our elites were expected to meet the enemy themselves, to fight with sword and lance in hand-to-hand combat. Any king who would not lead his men into battle was considered a coward and quickly deposed. Today our elite hide in bunkers, and even their men run robots that do all the fighting for them. What kind of chickenshits fight with drones, missiles, and robots? Many of the generals have never been in combat themselves; some of them have never even been in a bar room fight. The elites have designed terror weapons designed to wipe out huge populations if not most life in decade-long nuclear winters, while they hide in their plush bunkers dug deep into the eastern mountains. Chickenshits!! Cowards!!"

Hobbs had a lot more unpleasant things to say about our leaders; but I had recorded enough to give a good idea of his military ideas, which seemed to have a definite reactionary caste. He seemed to think knives and clubs were the ideal weapons.

FIFTEEN

It was peaceful again in my office. I spent days filling out the expungement papers and meditating on the picture of Yosemite. I also decided to read some detective novels since I could find nothing about the science or art of being a campus dick anywhere else. I could see from the novels that I needed to be a tough guy with a pistol hid under my coat, a blackjack in my back pocket, and a smart-ass comment ready for all occasions on my tongue.

I received a phone call from Jason ordering Joe and I to his office to talk about selling drones to the college and the local police. My girl friend Meridee was acting as the receptionist in Jason's office at the time, which gave me a chance to talk to her. Actually we had nearly an hour waiting for or on Jason, who was puffing up like a horned toad from his phony importance as drone dean. Joe immediately broke into my conversation with Meridee.

"Say," said Joe, "I understand you've kicked the shit out of Molly at the Racket Nest."

81

"Yes," murmured Meridee, "it was the only lady-like thing to do. She blew her nose on my hair."

"I had to pull her off your boy-friend. She was kicking the shit out of him, even broke a couple of ribs," said Joe. I just hung my head; I couldn't think of anything tough or smart-ass to say. I spent the next half-hour or so thinking of tough or smart-ass things to say. Finally Jason condescended to recognize our existence and appointment and let us into his office.

"Uncle Harry tells me we need to sell Sloan drones to campus security and to the city police department," said Jason.

"I have no budget for drones," I said, "I don't even have enough money for a snub-nosed Biretta or a black jack."

"No problem," said Jason, "I'll have the trustees and curators transfer a bunch of money out of faculty salaries into your budget."

"I have no idea how to operate the drones," I said.

"No problem," said Jason, "I'm giving drone lessons to Molly next week, and there's no reason why you can't join us."

"You're giving drone lessons to Molly!?" said Joe, who was clearly aghast at the idea.

"What's wrong with that?"

"Isn't that like giving the nuclear button to Donnie?"

"Donnie?"

"O never mind," said Joe realizing his place.

Finally I thought of something tough and smart-ass to say: "Why don't we change the name of the school to Sloan Drone Academy? Sounds a lot better than the University of Missouri at Deplorable City, don't you think?"

"No, I don't think so."

"No?"

"There's a famous economics professor who lives in New York who would be rather be professor of economics at the University of Missouri at Deplorable City than Leon Trotsky's godson," said Jason.

"Wow," said Joe, who was too young to remember the Commie menace, "He's Trotsky's godson, that's incredible."

"Besides," continued Jason, "this school has been the University of Missouri at Deplorable City for several decades now."

"Well," I said lamely, "they're renaming the streets and tearing down all those statues, so I thought it was a good idea."

"Be at the drone pavilion at 8 in the morning next Monday," Jason demanded.

By Wednesday Jason had transferred huge amounts of cash into the campus security account, and I was able to quickly transfer enough into my pocket to buy my pistol and blackjack before the bulk of the money was transferred to Sloan Manufacturing to pay for the new campus security drones. By Monday morning all the money was already gone, and half of the drones at the drone training field were under the control of campus security. Molly, Joe, Jason and I met at our drone hanger for our lesson.

I should have kept my mouth shut, but I just couldn't help it.

"What is she doing here?" I said to Jason, forgetting that he had invited her in the first place.

"I'm just as equal as you if not more so," Molly snarled.

"I thought she was in humanities or something like that."

"So what, asshole?" I could see she admired Dick Cheney too.

"I don't wrestle with pigs," I said. "You only get covered with shit and make the pig mad."

"Why you piece of shit," she said as she took a swing at me. However, I was ready for her. I stepped back out of her swing, grabbed the blackjack from my back pocket, and waved it in her face. Joe and Jason pulled us apart and calmed everything down.

It turned out the drones were controlled by electronic screens much like video games. Both Joe and Molly were very good at it; and their assigned drones destroyed the targets easily on the training ground just outside our hanger. I was not very good at it at all, and quickly lost control of my drone and crashed it in the Missouri river a few miles away.

"My god," I said, "this is awful. I'm sorry."

"Don't worry about it," said Jason, "I'll have a replacement sent out from the factory immediately."

"There's no more money in the budget."

"No problem. I'll put more money in your account from the teacher's funds. They make far too much money anyway."

SIXTEEN

Joe installed one of the drone screens in our office, and spent hours watching it as he flew one of our drones over the campus and the surrounding city. As a matter of fact, he began to spend more time at the drone screen than I spent meditating on the picture of Yosemite. I pointed out he was wasting too much time on the screen, that I thought he might just disappear one day into the screen and never come back; but he was adamant that it was the correct way to do the surveillance that was such an important part of our jobs as campus security.

At the same time I became aware of a subtle change in the campus atmosphere for the worse. There were flyers posted everywhere either promoting Paul Craig Robards coming speech promoting his White Dude Society or denouncing the campus administration for allowing a racist, male chauvinist pig like Robards to speak on campus. I took one of the anti-Robards flyers to Jason's office and asked him to reconsider allowing Robards' speech.

"Don't you believe in free speech?" Jason asked me.

"Of course, but on the other hand I don't think anyone should be allowed to scream fire in a crowded theater."

"So?" Evidently Jason was a fan of Dick Cheney too.

"We have an appointment with Captain Snarkel of the city police force to sell drones tomorrow. I want you and Joe Schultz to come with me since both of you knows how to operate the drones," Jason continued.

In the morning the three of us went to the hocus-pocus, Twelfth and Locust police station to meet Capt. Snarkel, a very large man full of bluster and bull. Jason presented our sales pitch to Snarkel, who seemed surprisingly unresponsive. Harry Sloan had told Jason that everything had been arranged through the Tucker law firm and the city council members who had been elected on Sloan's money.

"Well," blustered Snarkel, "we just had another police shooting, and you know how expensive that can be."

"Police shooting?" wondered Jason.

"Yes, one of our men shot someone running away from him and also hit three bystanders. Every time something like that happens it is very expensive; we have to expand our public relations campaign, and I think you know how expensive that can be," bulled Snarkel. Snarkel then excused himself for a moment to deal with a small emergency in the police office leaving the three of us wondering what the hell was happening. "I thought everything was set up," I said.

"Harry told me everything was already set up; but it appears we'll have to sell these damn things on their merits alone," complained Jason.

"I think he's looking for a bribe," said Joe, who turned out to be correct again. Jason slid some cash to Snarkel when he came back and promised him a set of season tickets in perpetuity to the local football games. Snarkel became very friendly and signed our papers immediately.

While Joe wired several police stations for drones I fell happily back into meditation and finishing my daily basis autobiography for the expungement papers. I hoped I would not be disturbed again; but soon the door on our office openly slowly and silently. There was no one opening the door, just a large Maine coon cat that strutted into the office and leapt up on my desk into the middle of my autobiography papers. It sat down in the middle of my autobiography and stared at me without blinking. I picked it up and threw it back into the hallway outside our office. A few minutes later the office door opened slowly and silently, the Maine coon cat strutted into my office, leapt up on my desk, sat down in the middle of my autobiography, and stared at me without blinking. I picked it up, threw it back into the hallway, and locked the office door behind me. I spent the rest of the day pleasantly meditating and writing about myself. What could be more fun?

Since Joe was out of the office I had to monitor the drone screen from time to time. Later that day I took a break by looking at the screen, which monitored the video from the drone we had continually circling over the campus. I saw something suspicious slinking across the main quadrangle, so I toggled the drone magnification up until I could see it was the Maine coon cat slinking away across the quadrangle.

Every now and then something uncanny seems to happen to me, something completely uncalled for, something almost beyond belief. I like a well-ordered life and existence, a life without surprises; but I am continually surprised as if an alternate reality kept trying to burst into my regulated and pleasant reality just to annoy me. Molly came out of the Humanities Building into the quadrangle, and the cat leapt into her outstretched arms. Even through the poor optics of the drone I could see they loved each other. Disgusting!!

At that disgusting moment Joe came back and looked over my shoulder at the monitor.

"Can you believe that?" I said.

"What?"

"Molly and that cat love each other."

"So?" I was getting tired of Joe continually copying Dick Cheney.

"That cat was just up here spying on us. Molly has trained the cat to spy on us."

"But Boss, you can't train a cat to do anything, much less spy on people."

"This is a special cat," I insisted, "It's a spy cat."

"How can the cat talk to Molly?" asked Joe. I must say, it was a perfectly reasonable question.

"Maybe she stuck a wire up its ass."

"Boss, you're just being paranoid."

"I'm just being reasonable."

"You think it's reasonable to suspect someone of sticking a wire up a cat's ass to spy on people?"

"Joe, it's the nature of our trade, our business. We have to be paranoid, we have to suspect everyone."

"I bet you don't believe Lee Harvey Oswald killed Kennedy, either."

"I sure don't. He was just a patsy; he said so himself. He was part of a conspiracy."

"Conspiracy?"

"Conspiracy!!"

"You believe in conspiracies?" said Joe.

"Yes, don't you?"

"Of course not," said Joe. This was the first instance I remember in which Joe's judgment appeared to be inferior to mine. I sometimes wondered why he was so much more competent than I was. I suspect it was because he had only a high school education and had not been stifled and dumbed with years of studying sociology and law.

SEVENTEEN

Joe decided we should look into the campus activities of the White Dude Club since they were so prominent in Molly's various pamphlets, posters, and her electronic hate mail we were monitoring. Although any target at all will suffice for hate; there's generally something in the target that draws the hate in the first place. There are a lot of things that aren't hated at all, and others that are hated by virtually everyone. Torture, for example, is hated by everyone but certain secret elements of our patriotic national security state.

At first I thought we would have to resort to infiltration and disguises to spy on the White Dudes Club; but one day I was recruited by a member of the Club, the Mr. Jaybird Bolton, who was also director of student loans who I had already met in my heroic defense of his office, which had been under attack from disgruntled debt slaves. Jaybird sported a full walrus moustache that hid his mouth completely; the moustache looked like a great impediment to eating, and a dangerous haven for mold, fungi, and God knows what else. But like so many grotesque features sported by grotesque people, it appeared to be dearly loved by Jaybird. He kept fiddling with it the entire time he talked to me, inviting to me to the daily meeting of the campus White Dude Club.

"Daily?" I said, "You meet daily?"

"Of course," said Jaybird, "Our business is of the utmost importance. Dick Jones, our great founder, started us on weekly meetings; but we quickly switched to daily meetings

I agreed to go the next day to their meeting at a coffee shop very close to the campus, but arrived late since their meetings started at 7 in the morning, which was very early for me. They all seemed to be arguing how much should be charged to use toilet paper.

"But there is no charge to use toilet paper," I said.

"Hey dude, every piece of white man's culture should have a user fee," said some dude with a bald head and a walrus moustache. I noticed everyone at the meeting except for myself sported a bald head and a walrus moustache.

"Yeah dude, remember what Paul Craig Robards said," Jaybird continued the thought, if it could be called a thought.

"What did Robards say?" I wondered.

"To pay for reparations to non-whites, whites need to charge non-whites to use our white civilization," said Jaybird.

"Yeah, dude. Smartphones, internet, cars, planes, European languages, electricity, magnets, firecrackers, gunpowder, and toilet paper."

"But dude," I said, "why charge non-whites user fees if the money just goes back to them anyway in reparations for past wrongs?"

"You don't understand, dude," said Jaybird.

Time had run out for the meeting, so I didn't get a chance to understand why I didn't understand. They finished the meeting with a curious ritual in which each dude thanked white dudes of the past for creating five different things. It was a thanksgiving, a chorus of gratitude. I couldn't think of anything white dude's had created because I began thinking about all the thefts, muggings, fights, diseases, deaths, gougings by the cartels that own everything, taxes for the perpetual wars, lies and hypocrisies flooding out of every T.V., the eternal dreck that pours over all of us, white or not. And perhaps most of us just want to go home, but there is no home in the Americas, and perhaps the reason we are here is because there was no home for us in Europe, Africa, or Asia either.

"Learn anything?" asked Joe as soon as I walked back into our office.

"Everyone in the White Dude's Club appears to be insane," I said.

"But we already knew that," said Joe.

"We didn't know exactly how insane they were."

"Well, how insane are they?"

"I think they're nuts enough to start a riot."

"Speaking of riots, read this from the Assistant Director of Student Financial Aid," said Joe, handing me a note in an envelope marked URGENT.

I read the note and said, "Another riot? Why?"

"I was just over there talking to the him. He told me a group of disgruntled alumni had invaded his office this morning and threatened him with various forms of murder and mayhem."

"Murder and mayhem? Why?"

"They can't find jobs and can't make their payments on their student loans."

"Why don't they take bankruptcy?"

"They can't."

"Why not?"

"Their student loans are all backed by the federal government, which insists no student debtor can have access to bankruptcy. These alumni told the Assistant Director they'll be back with gasoline and dynamite."

"I think this is a case for Jaybird Bolton; the Assistant works for him. Besides, what kind of alums are these? Where's their school spirit?"

"At any rate, the Assistant wants us to post a platoon of men at his office to guard against the alums."

At that point I remembered I still had large outstanding loans with that student loan office, and that I couldn't take bankruptcy either, something I had been very successful in repressing in my mind. I hate to brag, but only someone who is very good at meditation could ever have success repressing an ugly fact like that. I had also conveniently forgotten it was impossible to get a good paying job with my very expensive degree in sociology from the college.

"I think it's a job for the city police," I said.

"Snarkel?"

"Snarkel. Maybe we can get Jason to slip Snarkel more cash."

"Why?, asked Joe, "it's part of his job."

"Well, it was when the college was a city college, but it's a state college now."

"I don't see why you have to bribe Snarkel," said Joe.

"But you have to apply a little money to get anything done in this city."

"Why should it be that way?"

"Well, of course it shouldn't be that way," I said. Joe certainly was naïve. I decided to do nothing about the situation. I must admit I secretly longed for someone to burn down that student loan office.....financial aid, my ass.

EIGHTEEN

I sat with Meridee in front of the big screen at the Racket Nest watching the thin crowds of derelicts drift down Broadway from nowhere to nowhere; it wasn't nearly as pleasant as looking at the big picture of Yosemite going around the corner in its frame in my office, but at least I was away from work, I was no longer doing my duty as a campus dick.

"Did you know Molly comes into Jason's office all the time?" asked Meridee, who worked as an administrative assistant for Jason.

"No," I said, "but Joe, my assistant thinks she's setting the fires and bombs in the science buildings. He thinks we should bring her in for interrogation."

""I'd love to be there for an interrogation of her," grinned Meridee.

"I don't think that would be ethical."

"Do you think it's ethical to let her run amok?"

"Well, no."

"Did you know she comes into Jason's office virtually every day, criticizes whatever he's wearing, whatever is on his desk, his smell; and then forces him to commit degenerate, dirty acts right there in his office?"

"How do you know?"

"I hear everything and had the misfortune to walk in on them once."

"O," I mumbled.

"Why don't you do something?"

"Well, she's Jason's girlfriend."

"So?" My god, I couldn't believe it; Meridee appeared to be a fan of Cheney too.

"It's not my business."

"When she blew her nose on my hair I knocked the shit out of her; why don't you do something?"

"She's Jason's girl friend," I repeated, "it's up to Jason to do something."

"She has Jason wrapped around her little finger. You know what I think?"

"What?"

"I think you're a chickenshit. What kind of campus dick are you?"

"You know she's out of her mind."

"So?" There it was again, the cutting, brutal Cheney 'so'.

This was not the first time I've had this problem, with people insisting I do something, that I resort to actions whose consequence might very well be disastrous. I believe in letting things work themselves out; I believe in going with the flow; however this does not mean I'm not a tough guy.

"I don't believe in men picking on women," I said.

"I don't know what men and women have to do with this; that's not the issue."

"What's the issue?"

"Why are you such a chickenshit?"

"I am not a chickenshit. I'm actually a very tough guy who happens to believe discretion is the better part of valor."

Meridee told me I was making her sick; and that she had to leave, which she did. It was just as well since I received an urgent call from Joe who was still in our office. He said Jaybird Bolton had called and wanted protection in picking up Paul Craig Robards at the Charles P. Wheeler downtown airport for his campus speech sponsored by the White Dude's Club, and that someone, he suspected Molly, had splashed paint and egg on the campus statue of George Washington. In addition Joe said the Financial Aid Office appeared to be frantic with fear of a student attack, and that Molly was currently bullhorning the quadrangle with an outrageous, inflammatory rant.

I could see it was going to continue being a very bad day. As I walked to the campus police car, a distraught tomato walked past me yelling "Here asshole, come here ass hole." I cleverly deduced she had lost her dog with the unusual name. She turned to me and said:

"Have you seen my asshole?"

"Not yet," I had said as politely as possible. She gave me a truly evil-eye glare.

Now I could see I had to return quickly to the campus to deal with a very ugly situation. I walked into our office and found Joe close to hysteria.

"For God's sakes, where have you been?" said Joe.

"I took an extended nooner at the Racket Nest," I said. Joe did not drink anymore and was very self-righteous about his prized abstinence.

"What?" he said.

"I was unexpectedly detained," I said. I found it degrading to come up with excuses for someone who was my subordinate.

"We need to do something right away."

"All right," I said, "where's my gun?" I started going through the drawers of my desk.

"Here," Joe said, handing it to me in the correct fashion, grip first. I had never carried the thing before and didn't know what to do with it. Finally I stuck it in over my belt.

"Don't you have a holster for that pistol?" asked Joe.

"Holster?"

"Look, I have a holster for my gun that fits neatly under my armpit; with my jacket on it doesn't even look like I'm carrying."

"This is O.K."

"Do you have the safety on?"

"Safety?"

"There's a little lever or button on every gun that ensures it doesn't go off by mistake. You don't want to blow your dick off, do you?"

"Good God no, tough guys don't blow their dicks off.

NINETEEN

Molly was whipping her crowd in the quadrangle into a frenzy; none of them even noticed Joe and I joining the crowd.

"And those idiots are right here on this campus hiding out in the science buildings. First they invent atomic weapons, then they invent robots and A.I.. They invent all kinds of diabolical machines designed to get rid of all of us. They are idiots who pretend to be smart. Are any physicists really smart?" roared Molly through her bullhorn.

"Physicists are idiots" roared the crowd back at her.

"Chemists invent all kinds of poisonous compounds that flood our lands and seas. Are any chemists really smart?"

"Chemists are idiots," roared the crowd.

"Engineers build all kinds of cities that don't work, bridges to nowhere, and roads to oblivion. Are any engineers really smart?"

"Engineers are idiots!"

"Mathematicians stick their heads up their asses and never see the light of day again. Are any mathematicians really smart?"

As this point in Molly's harangue Jaybird Bolton tapped me on the shoulder and demanded I accompany him to the Charles P. Wheeler downtown airport to protect him and his guest, Paul Craig Robards. I left Molly's boiling mad crowd and drove down to the downtown airport to pick up Robards, who was scheduled to give a campus-wide speech at the Student Union at 5:00 that afternoon. The White Dude's Club had contracted with Executive Beechcraft to fly Robards up from Florida and back. Robards was an older Southern gentleman with old fashioned manners who seemed delighted to be in Deplorable City, for some reason. Jaybird gushed all over the poor man, whose speech was titled "Why White Dudes Matter."

"What's really important?" Jaybird asked him as soon as we were back in the campus car. It was one of the most stupid, idiotic questions I have ever heard, but I held my tongue out of deference to Robards. Sometimes I surprise myself with my wise restraint and diplomacy; but I dearly wanted to tell Jaybird what a fucking idiot he was.

"Well," Robards began slowly, "I'm afraid our country is falling apart. Even colleges have fallen apart. The chancellor at the last college I visited had written her PhD. thesis on queers and video games. The title of her thesis was 'Genderqueers and Their Incredible Lack of Representation in Video Games'. What kind of scholarship is that? It's truly trash scholarship, only fitting a trash culture."

"What's genderqueer?" wondered Jaybird in his best moronic voice.

"Some kind of academic jargon," said Robards.

"We've let all these technicians run amok. No society in its right mind would have ever invented the A-bomb, much less actually use it. No society in its right mind would countenance the invention of spy devices used to monitor everyone," continued Robards.

"You mean computers?" I asked as I drove over the river and into the downtown area.

"Yes, and now those assholes and their computer applications in Monopoly Valley are taking over the entire economy. Technicians don't even have a real education; they're just clever tradesmen."

I found all of this hard to believe; Paul Craig Robards and Molly seemed to agree on virtually everything, yet Molly wanted to shut down his speech and was currently whipping up some kind of lynch mob in the quadrangle. Maybe she wanted to lynch Robards himself.

"We're having some difficulties on campus right now," I said.

"Difficulties?"

Just as I said 'difficulties' the ring tone on my new smart phone informed me that I had an urgent message from Joe who I had left watching Molly perform at the quadrangle.

"Excuse me," I said. I had to take the call because of its urgency, though I tended to despise anyone rude enough to interrupt a conversation with a miserable cell phone call, which usually involved extended discussions of a whole lot of nothing.

"Get back quick, Boss. Molly and a mob are headed for our drone hangar", said Joe.

"So?" I just couldn't help it; I just had to be a Dick Cheney tough guy kind of smart-ass.

"Don't you remember; Jason gave Molly instructions on flying the drones and firing their missiles and guns? It looks like her mob intends to drone all the engineering and science buildings."

"O No!!!"

"O Yes. And by the way, another mob of disgruntled alums is currently setting fire to the Financial Aid Building."

"Call Capt. Snarkel and get the police there immediately." I had to admit I heard the last disaster with a certain amount of bittersweet joy, just a pinch of Schadenfreude. Perhaps my loan records would go up in the smoke.

"I've already called him; and he's activated his drone force and sent a platoon of cops to campus."

By this time we were close enough to the campus to see the glow of a massive fire against the clouds.

"Let me take you back to the airport," I said to Robards, "I don't think it would be a very good idea to give a talk at our campus today."

"What?!!" exclaimed Jaybird.

"The campus is under attack," I said.

"You can't do this," snarled Jaybird as I drove into a parking lot to turn around and go back to Charles P. Wheeler.

"The hell I can't!" I was really getting fed up with Jaybird Bolton and his impressive idiocy and arrogance.

"Aren't you a member of the White Dude's Club?" demanded Jaybird.

"So?" I asked, depending on the wisdom of Dick Cheney again.

"A white dude should not be a chickenshit like you," said Jaybird.

TWENTY

"Why you jerk," I said to the idiot, "do you want to get us all killed for nothing?"

"It's for the principle of the thing," said Jaybird without explaining what either the principle or the thing was. At this point Robards intervened and insisted on proceeding to the campus in spite of the disturbances because he didn't want to turn tail. I would have been more than happy to turn tail myself. By the time we reached the campus the battle was at a high pitch. Snarkel's police and the fire department were fighting the alums burning the student loan offices, and had brought in the police drones, which Sloan had supplied with incendiary missiles. Molly and her forces had already hit the engineering building and the chemistry building where Joe and I had our office with some of the school's drone missiles. Most of the campus buildings appeared to be on fire.

I pulled into the physics building's parking lot and began to pick up sniper fire shattering the windshield and punching holes in the car.

"Good God," said Jaybird, "I'm out of here!!" He leapt out of the car and ran off somewhere into the smoking and burning ruins. Fortunately about the same time Jaybird disappeared, Joe ran up to the car. I told Joe to take Robards to the Student Union where he was scheduled to give his speech "Why White Dudes Matter" in an hour, and wait for me there.

Joe had compiled a list of all the GPS co-ordinates for all the buildings on campus; and, as far as I knew I had the only list of co-ordinates in my desk in our office. I was determined to retrieve the list, and dodged about from burning building to burning building, trying to stay out of the line of fire of Molly's snipers.   But there was nothing left of the chemistry building but piles of rubble. I was poking around in the rubble wondering where my desk might be when someone said.

"What's going on here?" I turned around and spotted a large goon shaped man hulking through the smoke.

"Who the hell are you?"

"Mattis, F.B.I.", he said slipping open a badge.

"What do you want?" I demanded.

"This is my jurisdiction; we were afraid the local low-level civil war around here would accelerate into an insurrection."

"This is my jurisdiction, I'm head of campus security."

"Then you have to take orders from me; I represent D.C. itself."

"Bullshit," I said. I was really getting mad; however, at the same time I had spotted the remnants of the picture of Yosemite poking up through a pile of rubble.

"I would be ashamed to admit I was head of campus security, if I were you," continued the goon. I ignored him and began to dig around in the rubble where I had spotted Yosemite, hoping to find my desk.

"Did you hear me?" he continued. I had immediate luck and found both my desk and the list of co-ordinates in its upper drawer.

"I represent D.C.; our law is superior to any local law," he said.

"Your agency and some of the other government agencies are the reason Deplorable City is deplorable," I said. He didn't reply; he folded up and hit the ground.

I went over to him and put my hand on his neck. He appeared to be dead already; hit by sniper fire. I hurried away towards the Student Union building to retrieve Paul Craig Robards and Joe while transmitting the co-ordinates up to Snarkel in the command police helicopter. However, from the damage that had already been done to the social science and humanities buildings it appeared Snarkel already had some co-ordinates to feed into the Chinese guidance systems on Sloan's missiles. I found Robards and Joe in front of the Student Union. As I suspected, Joe had already given Snarkel the GPS co-ordinates of all the buildings on campus. Robards wondered what had happened to Jaybird Bolton, the sponsor of his trip to campus.

"I don't know; I haven't seen him since he ran away," I said.

"Would you tell him next time you see him that I had to return to Florida, and apologize for me?" said Robards.

"Apologize?"

"I don't think it would be a good idea to attempt a speech in this atmosphere."

"I don't think there's any reason to apologize to Jaybird Bolton. Let's retrieve the campus police car, get back to the airport, and get you out of Deplorable City."

We were able to do it, though the ride back to the airport was certainly breezy with no windshield. It was a kind of triumph, although the last triumph for the campus police of the University of Missouri at Deplorable City. By the time Joe and I returned to campus the battle was over. No one had won; but the campus was demolished.

A few months later we found that the great state of Missouri, never much a patron of scholarship and learning, had decided not to rebuild the campus. The University of Missouri at Deplorable City was gone, dissolved and hidden in the mists of a past that continue to confuse and confound us today.

THE END.